THE AIGAS C(

D0581081

The Aigas Cookbook

by

Lucinda Lister-Kaye

with drawings by
Heather Cary

Aigas Books
Beauly
Inverness-shire
IV4 7AD

First published 1999

Printed by Highland Printers
Inverness

I dedicate this little book to the principal recipients of its contents, the seven children of my family: Warwick, James, Amelia, Melanie, Emma, Hamish and Hermione.

~

Cook's Acknowledgements

This is a collection of recipes which I have used successfully over many years at Aigas. In some instances their origins are lost to me in the steamy haze of culinary time; others, I know, came down to me from my mother, Anne Law, who taught me to cook as a child. Later I trained, and finally taught at, the Cordon Bleu Cookery School in Marylebone Lane, London. I am very grateful to my mother, as I am to all my large family, for the essential ingredients of encouragement and enthusiastic appetite liberally sprinkled in over the years.

My thanks, too, go to my good friend Lady Claire Macdonald of Macdonald who has made such a success of Highland cooking through her own books and her now world famous Kinloch Lodge Hotel on the Isle of Skye. Six of these recipes are, but for minor titillations which have evolved in the Aigas kitchens, essentially hers. Similarly, other cooks at Aigas over the years have left a legacy of ideas and innovations, some of which are included here. I acknowledge all of these with much gratitude.

My son Hamish is now also a trained cook who studied under the celebrated Irish cook, Darina Allen, at Ballymaloe near Cork. His skills have been tested on all of us. It was wonderful to be able to ask him to check through the text for errors, and include his recipe ideas as well. It makes it a real family effort.

Our friend and neighbour Heather Cary, well known for her animal portraits, has produced the illustrations. I am especially grateful to her for these friendly sketches.

Finally, it is Lindsey Stout in the Aigas office to whom I owe special thanks for typesetting, planning and proof-reading this manuscript, as well as tasting and sampling kitchen offerings, especially baking, which from time to time mysteriously appear among the files and computers of the office.

Lady Lister-Kaye
House of Aigas

Foreword

There was a time when I was happy with a tin of baked beans and half a pound of sausages. In those days, as an incurable out-doorsman, camping and roughing it right round the northern hemisphere, food was a necessity to be prepared and consumed with as little trouble as possible - although, come to think of it, that's not quite true. Even in the high Arctic, camping on ice and permafrost in the dead of winter, beneath shimmering stars and with the northern lights pulsating overhead, I well remember insisting that the sausages were a little burnt in the crackling camp fire, and the beans, crisping to one side of the tin in the hot embers, to be scraped off later as a bonus; camp specialities one would find hard to emulate in a kitchen; a special delicacy which fixes the place and the moment as well as just tasting good.

It is not surprising, then, that thirty years later I should still consider cooking to be as much to do with the occasion as the food itself. The recollection of great dinners in uplifting company returns to me whenever I taste certain special dishes. So to be married to a cook who not only enjoys cooking - she seems to make it effortless, like a musician at one with her instrument - but who has also featured as my hostess on so many great occasions, makes eating a doubly pleasurable experience.

Aigas has been our home for many years, and it is also a working estate and Field Centre. Visitors and friends from all over the world have sat down with us and our family to enjoy these dishes.

I have been given the pleasing task of writing an introduction to each section to reflect the family's involvement in my wife's cooking. We both hope that from this little book you may be able to relive memories of the House of Aigas and create new ones of your own.

Sir John Lister-Kaye
House of Aigas

Measurements

These recipes have been collected over a period of years and span the change from imperial to metric measurements. A conversion table is included in the appendix. Where conversions were given in the original recipes they are duplicated. I have not tried to convert each recipe because exact conversions from metric to imperial and vice versa are impossible to achieve on kitchen scales. If in doubt, bear in mind that the proportions of ingredients should be similar, rather than trying to calculate strictly accurate conversions.

Contents

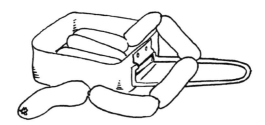

Contents

Contents

Contents

Starters

~

In the 1980s Iona Noble came to cook for us at Aigas. She was an Earth Mother, with a baby on her aproned hip as she whisked home-collected honey into home-made yoghurt and sieved cheeses from her own hand-milked goats. She calmly turned our traditional notion of home-cooking on its head. We had to put locks on the larder doors to prevent Field Centre staff from tip-toeing down in the night for her sticky flapjacks or cheesy dips and crudités.

One of her innovations which has been universally popular for fifteen years is the unlikely combination of grapefruit and onion salad seasoned with a piquant vinaigrette. It is fresh, tangy and palate-tingling as a summer starter, perfect for warm weather, as is her spinach roulade, alas no longer made with her own cream cheese.

Iona left us to have another baby and to run her own guesthouse on the West Coast. I went to see her once. There were children everywhere, chickens on the doorstep, goats and ponies almost in the kitchen and shaggy dogs curled up against the Rayburn. Outside, only yards away, a gentle sea lapped at a shingle beach and the great Cuillin mountains surged upwards to a jagged horizon. I hope she is pleased that her recipes are still with us. We miss her.

The egg and onion ramekins and the ratatouille are Lucinda's favourite starters. I like them too hot to touch, and just enough to make you wish there were more.

Egg & Onion Casserole

(Serves 6)

Ingredients
6 eggs
4 onions
2 tbsp. butter
1/2 pint light béchamel sauce
salt and freshly ground black pepper

Method: Casserole

Hard-boil the eggs for fifteen minutes in boiling water. Remove shells and slice eggs. Slice onions and sauté in butter until they are soft and golden; do not let them brown. Add onions and butter to hot béchamel sauce; stir well; fold in the egg slices and season well with salt and freshly ground black pepper. Heat through in individual ramekins to serve.

Method: Béchamel Sauce

1/2 oz butter
1/2 oz flour
1/2 pt milk
1 onion
blade of mace
bay leaf
salt & pepper to taste

Bring milk to the boil with a slice of onion, salt, pepper, a blade of mace and a bay leaf as flavourings. Leave to cool.

Melt the butter, add the flour and cook for half a minute. Gradually add the milk, stirring continuously and slowly bringing to the boil. Boil for three minutes, stirring continuously to remove any lumps.

Grapefruit & Onion Salad

Ingredients
tinned or fresh grapefruit, peeled and sliced
thinly sliced onion
vinaigrette dressing

Method
Mix all together and display on a bed of lettuce. Sprinkle with chopped parsley.

Iona Noble used to serve this in a large dish liberally washed with vinaigrette from which people helped themselves, but we now serve this unusual but popular salad starter on individual plates with the grapefruit segments artfully arranged on the top. An excellent accompaniment for this dish would be the Rosemary Damper on page 62.

Ratatouille

Ingredients
8 tbsp. olive oil
2 Spanish onions, sliced
2 green peppers, cubed
2 aubergines, cubed or sliced (eggplant)
2 courgettes, cut in 1/2 inch (1 cm) slices
4-6 ripe tomatoes - peeled, de-seeded and chopped
salt and freshly ground black pepper
1 tbsp. chopped fresh parsley
pinch of marjoram or oregano
1 large clove garlic, crushed

Method

Heat the olive oil in a large frying pan, add the onion slices and sauté until they are transparent. Add the green peppers and aubergines and, five minutes later, the courgettes and tomatoes. The vegetables should not be fried but stewed in the oil, so simmer gently in a covered pan for thirty minutes. Season to taste with the salt and freshly ground black pepper and add the chopped parsley, marjoram, basil and crushed garlic then cook uncovered for about ten to fifteen minutes, or until the ratatouille is well mixed and has the appearance of a ragoût of vegetables – which it is. Serve hot from the casserole, or cold, as a delicious beginning to a summer meal.

Spinach Roulade

(Serves 6)

Ingredients: Roulade
1 1/2 oz butter
1 1/2 oz plain flour
4 oz frozen spinach
3/4 pint milk
3 eggs, separated
pinch nutmeg
salt and pepper

Ingredients: Filling
8 oz cream cheese
chives
2 tbsp. yoghurt
salt and pepper to taste

Method

Cook the spinach until tender, drain and finely chop in a blender. Line a swiss roll tin with baking parchment. Melt the butter and flour and stir in the milk, cooking gently until thick. Beat in the spinach, salt, pepper, nutmeg and egg yolks. Whisk the egg whites until stiff and fold in lightly. Pour into tin. Bake for about ten to fifteen minutes at 180°C/350°F/Gas Mark 4 until just firm. Take out of oven and cover with a damp cloth until ready to fill.

Turn out onto a fresh piece of baking parchment and spread with the filling, rolling carefully.

Cooling Summer Soups

~

Many of our friends live in hot climates: California, Florida, Texas, and parts of Australia and Africa. I can see these soups being popular there, although dear old Scotland can also produce dazzling June and July weather, like 1996, when the Field Centre Rangers never wore their waterproofs from May until October.

Summer soups make me think of dining in daylight, not candlelight. Here in the Highlands, Latitude 57° 30', north of Gothenburg and Moscow, we have twenty two and a half hours of daylight at the end of June. Dinner at eight o'clock can often mean strong evening sun glinting on the table silver, beaming arcs reflecting from wineglasses onto the ceiling. I think of bright damask tablecloths and Lily of the Valley and Iceberg Roses in crystal vases, chilled Chablis condensing on the outside of the glass. I don't know why, but I also think of Rupert Brooke's *The Great Lover:*

"These I have loved:
White plates and cups, clean gleaming,
Ringed with blue lines; and feathery aery dust;
Wet roofs beneath the lamp-light; the strong crust
Of friendly bread; and many-tasting food;
Rainbows; and the blue-bitter smoke of wood;
And radiant raindrops couching in cool flowers;
And flowers themselves, that sway through the sunny hours,
Dreaming of moths that drink them under the moon..."

Borscht

A Summer Soup

(Serves 6 to 8)

Ingredients
12 oz (350 g) cooked beetroot, peeled and grated
2 carrots, grated
1 onion, finely chopped
1 celery stalk, finely chopped
1 1/2 pints (850 ml) beef stock
strip of zest and 1 tbsp. of lemon juice
bouquet garni (celery/thyme/bay leaf/parsley)
6 fl oz (175 ml) sour cream
salt and freshly ground black pepper

Method

Put the beetroot in a large pan with the carrots, onion and celery. Stir in the stock, lemon zest and bouquet garni. Season with salt and pepper. Bring to the boil and then lower the heat. Cover and simmer for forty minutes.

Remove the lemon zest and bouquet garni. Purée the soup in batches, using a food processor or blender. Strain into a bowl or serving tureen and leave to cool. When the soup is completely cold, stir in the lemon juice and all but six tablespoons of the sour cream. Adjust the seasoning to taste and cover and chill for at least two hours. Swirl the reserved sour cream into the soup to serve.

Tomato, Orange & Basil Soup

May be served hot or cold

(Serves 6)

Ingredients
1 lb (500 g) tomatoes
2 oz (50 g) butter
2 medium-sized onions, peeled and chopped
1 stick of celery, sliced
1 large potato, peeled and chopped
a few strips of orange rind
a few sprigs of fresh basil or 1/2 rounded tsp. basil
11/4 pints (700 ml) chicken stock
1/4 pint (150 ml) fresh orange juice
salt and freshly ground black pepper
1/2 rounded tsp. sugar
6 tbsp. single cream

Method

Slice the tomatoes in half and remove as many of the seeds as possible. Melt the butter in a saucepan and add the chopped onion, celery and potato, cooking over a gentle heat until the onion is soft and transparent (remember to stir the pan to prevent the potato sticking). Add the tomatoes, orange rind, chicken stock, fresh orange juice, salt, pepper, sugar and dried basil (if using). Bring to the boil and simmer gently for half an hour or until the potato is well cooked. Remove from the heat and cool. Purée the soup using a blender - if you are using fresh basil, add it now. Check the seasoning and sieve into a serving bowl. Keep in the refrigerator and serve each bowlful with a spoonful of cream swirled into the centre.

For a new twist, add two tablespoons of marmalade.

Watercress & Lemon Soup

A Summer Soup

(Serves 6 to 8)

Ingredients
2 oz (50 g) butter
2 medium-sized onions, peeled and chopped
2 medium-sized potatoes, peeled and chopped
1 1/2 pints (850 ml) chicken stock
2 bunches watercress, washed and trimmed
1 tbsp. lemon juice
salt and freshly ground black pepper
1/4 pint (150 ml) single cream

Method

Melt the butter in a large saucepan, add the onions and cook gently for fiv
minutes. Add the potatoes and cook for another five minutes (remember t
stir the pot from time to time to prevent sticking). Add the chicken stocl
Chop a generous bunch of watercress and add to the stock, bringing to th
boil and simmering very gently for half an hour, or until the potato is we
cooked. Remove from the heat and allow to cool (once cooled, this soup ca
be kept in the refrigerator until needed). Purée the cooled soup using
blender or food processor. Stir in the lemon juice, salt and black pepper an
sieve the purée into a serving tureen.

Before serving, strip the leaves from the remaining bunch of watercress an
chop roughly. Stir into the cooled soup and swirl a spoonful of cream into th
centre of each plateful.

Warming Winter Soups

~

A winter soup should be a meal in itself, thick and bitty and with lots of flotsam floating around.

The Highland winters are dark and wet and cold. Dreich is the excellent local (Gaelic) word. To come in from working outside at lunch-time to a bowl of Cullen Skink accompanied by crusty granary bread cut in thick chunks, or cracked wheat rolls warmed in the Aga oven, is one of the great delights which make the six months of winter tolerable. In the darkest of those December or January days, the problem is getting back to work afterwards. The temptation to sit beside a crackling pine-log fire with a mug of tea and watch the short day dwindle to a dank close often proves to be irresistible.

Lucinda seems to have a stock-pot simmering on the Aga all winter. It is a Moloch of left-overs. Into its steamy murk go duck and pheasant carcasses, ham and venison bones, leeks and shredded cabbage. Red wine lees get tipped in, and sometimes Guinness, along with cold Brussels sprouts and bread sauce left over from Sunday lunch. The result, sometimes days later, is a delectable broth of indeterminate colour and no conceivable way of writing down the recipe. One just has to create these masterpieces oneself.

While those listed here are much more precise in concoction they, too, fill and warm both elegantly and with distinction. Perfect for winter.

Carrot & Cumin Soup

One of Hamish's favourite recipes, handed down from Darina Allen at Ballymaloe.

(Serves 6)

Ingredients
560 g (1 1/4 lb) carrots, chopped
115 g (4 oz) onion, chopped
130 g (5 oz) potatoes, chopped
40 g (1 1/2 oz) butter
1.2 l (2 pints) home-made chicken stock
65 ml (2 1/2 fl oz) creamy milk (optional)
3 tsp whole cumin seeds
salt & freshly ground black pepper, sugar

to garnish:- a little whipped cream or yoghurt
freshly roasted and ground cumin
coriander leaves

Method

Heat the cumin seeds in a frying pan, just for a minute or two until they smell rich and spicy. Grind in a pestle and mortar or a spice grinder. Melt the butter in a medium-sized saucepan. When it foams, add the chopped vegetables and the cumin seeds. Season with salt, pepper and a pinch of sugar. Cover with buttered greaseproof paper and a tight-fitting lid. Allow to sweat gently on a low heat for about ten minutes or until the vegetables have softened slightly. Remove the lid. Add the stock, increase the heat and boil until the vegetables are soft. Liquidize until smooth. Taste and adjust the seasoning, adding a little creamy milk if necessary.

To serve: garnish each portion with a blob of whipped cream or yoghurt, sprinkle with a little ground cumin and top with a coriander leaf.

Cream of Mushroom Soup with Marsala

(Serves 6)

Ingredients

1 1/2 oz (45 g) butter
1 1/2 lb (675 g) mushrooms, roughly chopped
1 shallot, finely chopped
1/2 garlic clove, chopped
2 tbsp. of flour
3 1/2 fl oz (100 ml) Marsala
1 1/4 pints (700 ml) well-flavoured chicken or vegetable stock
6 fl oz (175 ml) double cream
salt and freshly ground black pepper
chopped flat-leaf parsley or chervil, to garnish

Method

Melt the butter in a large heavy-based saucepan. Add the mushrooms, shallots and garlic and cook, stirring, for four minutes. Stir in the flour and continue cooking for one minute. Gradually stir in the Marsala and stock. Season and bring to the boil, then lower the heat, cover and simmer for twenty minutes.

Purée the soup in a blender or food processor, in batches if necessary, until smooth and return it to the pan. Just before serving, stir in all but four tablespoons of the cream and heat the soup through gently. Adjust the seasoning and serve garnished with swirls of the reserved cream and parsley or chervil to garnish.

(Note: if available, field mushrooms will give a much better flavour than cultivated ones. A mixture of mushroom varieties is best, particularly if it includes a few ceps)

Cullen Skink

A Traditional, Warming Soup

(Serves 4 to 6)

Ingredients
1 smoked haddock
boiling water as required
1 tbsp. minced onion
1 pint single cream
salt and black pepper to taste
mashed potato as required
1 oz (30 g) butter

<u>Method</u>

Cook and mash some potato and set aside. Carefully skin the smoked haddock and place in a saucepan. Add enough boiling water to cover and bring slowly to the boil. Add the onion and cover and simmer gently until the flesh comes easily away from the bone, then remove haddock and slip all the flesh away from the bones. Flake fish and return bones to stock. Simmer for forty-five minutes, then strain. Bring to the boil once again. Meanwhile, bring the milk to the boil in a separate saucepan and stir it into the stock, then add the flaked fish. Season to taste with salt and pepper. Simmer for a minute or two, then gradually stir in enough mashed potato to give a creamy consistency. Add the butter a little at a time, stirring between each addition and bringing the soup to the boil.

Garnish with a heaped teaspoon of finely chopped chives or parsley. (To vary, stir two tablespoons of cream into the soup before serving.)

MAIN COURSES

Beef

~

We're fussy about beef - or perhaps a better word is spoilt. For twenty-five years we have bred our own pedigree Highlanders, shaggy, long-horned, gentle beasts which have evolved in this landscape of mountain and moor for as long as people have been here. Some say that they are the domesticated descendants of the great aurochs, the European wild ox, sadly long extinct, which features so lyrically on the smoky cave walls of Altamira and Lascaux.

They mature slowly; half as long again as modern commercial cattle because, for centuries, their rumbly intestines have had to cope with woody heather stems, pithy rushes and the tender shoots of eared willow as well as rank and un-nutritious mountain grasses. For that reason their meat is "marbled" with veins of fat running through the muscle, and it possesses a dark gamey colour and an unforgettably moorland flavour.

When we kill a stirk (bullock) for the pot, we ask the butcher to hang the carcase for a week; a natural tenderising process which obviates the need for the chemical treachery employed elsewhere. The result is something very distinctive: a steak as dark as a peaty lochan, the delicate essence of which seems to relive the summer scents of heather and bog myrtle, rushes and shady birch hollows.

You don't have to have Highland cattle to enjoy Aigas Bourguignon, but the steak must be tender and diced not too small. The marinade is vital. It is a classic dish, this, one which never fails to please and satisfy. It is fun, too, to do what Lucinda does to give it the personal touch. She tinkers with the seasonings for the marinade by making up her own special bouquets garni from local aromatic herbs and spices, no two of which are ever quite the same.

An old Highland saying: *"There's aye water where the stirkie droons"*. (There's always water where the bullock drowns – there's never smoke without fire.)

Not long after we married Lucy's introduction to Highlanders was an adventure. We farmed on the flood plain of the River Glass. Every year the valley flooded when a mild west wind from the Atlantic thawed the deep snowfields high in the Affric hills. On those wet meadows full of wild flowers we ran seventy Highland cows and a bull called Tearlach (Gaelic for Charlie).

One April morning the police phoned to say that the river was bursting its banks and we had better get the livestock to safety. By the time we got there it was too late. The fields were an angry sea of brown surging water, already several feet deep. All the cattle were huddled together on the high ground near the road except for a few which were stranded on an island ridge of dry land two hundred and fifty yards away, out across the water. We rushed off to get a boat. The torrent continued to rise.

When we returned the cattle were up to their bellies in water, looking miserable and belling loudly. I rowed towards them, Lucy standing in the bows with a rope. Eight times we approached those cows and seven times the current swept us aside. At last, after more than an hour in the icy lashing rain, somehow she managed to get a noose around the wide horns of a favourite old cow called Mairi Pollock. Gently we coaxed her into the deep water, towing her as she swam, Lucy pulling on the rope and urging her on all the way. As we hoped they would, the others gingerly followed her until, at last, the horned heads of all fourteen cattle, mouths open, nostrils flaring, were swimming strongly on either side of the boat. It took us nearly another hour to reach high ground, half a mile downstream. Later that night, over a large whisky I heard Lucy recount the tale to a friend. "This is not really the sort of farming I'm used to," she said.

Aigas Beef Bourguignon

(Serves 4)

Ingredients
2 1/2 lb beef
1/2 lb unsmoked bacon
1/2 lb carrots, sliced
12 baby carrots
12 button mushrooms
12 button onions
2 ounces onion, finely chopped
1 ounce shallots, finely chopped
2-4 cloves garlic
1 tbsp. flour
butter
1/2 bottle red wine
1 glass water
1-2 sprigs thyme
1-2 bay leaves
bouquet garni (celery, thyme, bay leaf, parsley)
salt and freshly ground black pepper

Method

Cut the beef into bite-sized pieces and marinate overnight in red wine with the carrots, shallots, onion, thyme and bay leaves. Drain well and dry lightly with a clean cloth. Dice the bacon and brown with small onions and carrots. When these are lightly coloured, remove them together with the bacon and sauté the drained beef in the remaining fat until brown. Sprinkle with flour and add the red wine from the marinade and a glass of water. Return the diced bacon, onions and carrots to the pan and add garlic and a bouquet garni; season to taste with salt and freshly ground black pepper. Simmer gently until meat is tender and the sauce reduced to half the original quantity - about three hours. Brown the mushrooms in butter and add to the meat about ten minutes before the end of the cooking time.

Beef & Guinness Pie

Guinness lends a unique taste to this dish but if it is not available, any other stout may be used instead.

(Serves 4)

Ingredients
675 g / 1 1/2 lb braising steak, cubed
12 baby onions, peeled
450 g / 1 lb puff pastry
2 tbsp. flour
1/2 tsp. mustard powder
4 tbsp. olive oil
250 ml / 8 fl oz Guinness or other stout
250 ml / 8 fl oz beef stock
sprig of thyme
2 tsp. Worcestershire Sauce
1 egg, beaten
milk, to glaze
salt
freshly ground black pepper

Method

Sieve the flour, mustard powder, salt and pepper together into a mixing bowl. Toss the meat in the seasoned flour and set aside. Heat the oil in a flameproof oven dish or a heavy-based pan over a high heat and brown the onions. Remove the onions and set aside. Brown the meat in batches, stir in the Guinness, stock, thyme and Worcestershire sauce. Bring to the boil, cover and simmer for a couple of hours or until the meat is tender.

With about half an hour of the cooking period to go, preheat the oven to 220°C/425°F/Gas Mark 7 and stir the onions into the meat mixture, removing the sprig of thyme. Dampen the edge of the pie dish with water and cut a long strip of pastry, which will hold the lid of the pie in place. Once you have edged the pie dish, dampen the top of the pastry strip and make a pastry lid for the pie, crimping it into place. Fill the empty pie dish, making sure that there is more meat in the centre than at the edges to hold up the pastry during cooking. Remember to make a slit in the centre of the lid to allow the steam to escape during cooking and brush the pastry with the beaten egg and a little milk to glaze. Use the pastry trimmings to decorate the pie and apply another coat of glaze.

Bake the pie in the oven for half an hour or until the pastry is well risen and golden brown.

MAIN COURSES

Chicken

~

God was not kind to the chicken. It is an unenviable lot, the hen's. From the moment of hatching to final arrival at the great celestial granary, she is not only prey for just about everything with sharp teeth or claws, but her eggs are filched from beneath her bottom and she has so little brain that taking evasive action when the awful moment comes never seems to occur to her until it is too late.

We can't keep hens. Note the verb: can't, not don't. We do, normally about twenty mixed Rhode Island Reds and Aberdeen Rangers, with a cockerel and a few Bantams thrown in for Hermione, but they are ephemeral. They pass through Aigas like passage migrants, transmogrifying involuntarily from witless but happy free-range worm-peckers to something's next meal; a tell-tale "broken hand" of mangled pinions discovered beneath a rhododendron bush by the Jack Russell terriers. We can't keep them from being gobbled by foxes, wildcats, pine martens (especially pine martens), passing otters and toothless, grumpy old badgers, upon whose regular circuit the hen run certainly features large. It is the price we inevitably pay for living up a glen among the mountains and forests of some of the most breath-catching scenery in Britain. We would not change it.

The trouble is our latitude again. Too much darkness in winter; hens are caught out in the paddock in the four o'clock gloaming by a bold fox, or, staying out too late in the slanting sun of a June evening, are snatched by a pine marten which couldn't wait for the brief midnight darkness. And then, every once in a while, disaster strikes. Somebody forgets to lock them up at night. The pine marten which lives in the stables roof only a few yards away, and which must check us out nightly, finds an open invitation to dinner. He can bring his friends too - and he does. We are lucky if any survive such a whirlwind of predatory devastation, so we just go on buying replacements which last a few months (or a couple of years if they're very lucky), while we enjoy their gloriously sunset-orange yolks in our scrambled egg.

Would that some more of the world's hens could enjoy the brief meadow-scratching innocence of our hens' lives.

Cape Chicken

Courtesy of Janice Bunce. Janice cooked at Aigas for several years. We have loved the South African influence she has brought to our menus.

(Serves 16 to 20)

Ingredients
20 pieces chicken
40 pitted prunes
110 g (4 oz) bottle capers (reserve some juice)
110 g (4 oz) bottle green olives
5 large cloves garlic, crushed
200 ml (7 fl oz) red wine vinegar
200 ml (7 fl oz) olive oil
salt and freshly milled black pepper
10 ml (1/2 fl oz) dried oregano
10 bay leaves
150 ml (5 fl oz / 1/4 pint) brown sugar
375 ml (13 fl oz) dry white wine
125 ml (4 fl oz) finely chopped parsley

Method

Arrange the chicken in an ovenproof dish and dot evenly with the prunes, drained capers and olives. Mix the garlic, vinegar, oil and a little caper juice and whisk and pour over the chicken. Season with salt and pepper and sprinkle with oregano. Cover and refrigerate overnight.

Next day, preheat oven to 180°C/350°F/Gas Mark 4. Turn the chicken, placing the prunes, capers and olives under the chicken. Sprinkle with brown sugar and pour the wine carefully in at one corner of the dish. Bake, uncovered, low down in the oven for fifty or sixty minutes until done, basting frequently with the pan juices. Skim and pour off the excess fat. Serve on a bed of rice moistened with the pan juices and sprinkled with parsley.

Coronation Chicken

(Serves 6-8)

For this recipe the chicken can either be roasted or poached (whole chicken or breast only). The ingredients for preparing a whole chicken are given below.

Ingredients
1 chicken
700 ml (1 1/4 pints) mayonnaise
15 ml (1/2 fl oz) paprika
45 ml (1 1/2 fl oz) medium curry powder
dash of Tabasco Sauce
salt
ground black pepper

to serve:-
rice
currants
cooked peas

Method

Cut the chicken into strips. Mix all the ingredients together and spoon over the chicken. To serve, lay on a bed of rice with the currants and the cooked peas. Sprinkle with roast almonds before serving.

Creamy Chicken & Broccoli

(Serves 6)

The sauce for this dish includes mayonnaise which, while sounding rather odd, is quite delicious. The advantage of this recipe is that it can be prepared several hours in advance and re-heated when necessary. The vegetables are cooked in with the chicken and the sauce, making vegetable side dishes unnecessary. May be served with rice or potatoes.

Ingredients
4 lb (1.8 kg) chicken
1 onion, peeled and quartered
1 carrot, peeled and cut into chunks
bouquet garni (celery, thyme, bay leaf, parsley)
some black peppercorns
freshly ground black pepper
salt
2 lb (900 g) frozen broccoli
butter for greasing
2 oz (50 g) butter
2 oz (50 g) plain flour
1 rounded tbsp. curry powder
7 oz (200 g) tin evaporated milk
4 tbsp. mayonnaise
2 tbsp. lemon juice
2 oz (50 g) Cheddar cheese, grated

Method

Cover the chicken with water and add the onion, carrot, bouquet garni, salt and peppercorns. Bring to the boil, cover and simmer gently for an hour or until the juices run clear when a skewer is inserted into the thigh. Leave to cool in the pan with the stock.

Separately, boil or steam the broccoli until the stalks are just tender. Drain and refresh under running cold water. Butter a large, shallow 3 pint (1.7 litre) ovenproof dish and arrange the drained broccoli on the bottom. When the chicken has cooled enough to handle, remove it from the stock. Reserve and sieve the stock. Skin and de-bone the carcase, spreading strips of the meat evenly over the broccoli.

Warm the butter in a saucepan and stir in the flour and curry powder. Fry over a gentle heat for one to two minutes, then gradually stir in 1 pint (600 ml) of the chicken stock. Stir rapidly until the sauce boils. Remove from the heat and add the evaporated milk, mayonnaise, lemon juice and grated cheese, continuing to stir until the cheese has melted. Check the seasoning and add some salt and pepper if necessary. Pour the sauce over the chicken in the dish.

Bake in a moderately hot oven at 190°C/375°F/Gas Mark 5 for half an hour or until the sauce is just bubbling.

Hamish's Chicken Casserole

(Serves 6-8)

Ingredients

1 chicken weighing about 3 1/2 lb (1.5 kg)
1 1/2 oz (40 g) butter
3 tbsp. Grand Marnier
3 tbsp. chicken stock
8 fl oz (250 ml) double cream
1 oz (25 g) flaked toasted almonds
4 medium cooking apples
1 1/2 oz (40 g) butter

Method: Chicken

Divide chicken into six portions and coat in seasoned flour. Heat the butter in a heavy frying pan and fry the chicken until it is a golden brown all over. Sprinkle with 2 tablespoons of Grand Marnier and add the stock. Cover tightly and cook for thirty minutes or until tender. Remove the chicken to a serving dish and keep warm. Add the remaining Grand Marnier and the cream to the pan, scooping up the brown bits from the bottom. Stir gently until heat through (do not boil), adjust the seasoning to taste and spoon over the chicken. Serve garnished with apples and sprinkled with flaked almonds.

Method: Apple Garnish

Peel, core and slice the apples. Place in a shallow baking dish in one layer. Pour over melted butter and bake in a pre-heated oven at 180°C/350°F/Gas Mark 4 for fifteen minutes or until the apples are soft. Use the garnish while hot.

MAIN COURSES

Fish
~

Salmon and trout inevitably feature in an Aigas cookbook. Every summer the Atlantic salmon swim past us to spawn in the headwaters of the River Glass. This majestic fish has been an essential component of the sporting economy of this glen for the past two hundred years. Just as the fish migrate in from the sea, so their dedicated fishers migrate north from the more densely populated regions of the U.K. We always know the fishermen by their Volvo estates or Range Rovers parked along the river from June onwards, rod clips attached to roofs and bonnets. People pay serious money to catch salmon in the Highlands.

Trout, on the other hand, are the fish of the people. The brown trout, which is the native freshwater fish here, is found in every burn and loch as well as in the rivers. Dunc Doolie, now in his late seventies, who has lived here man and boy and knows the river better than most, tells me that in his youth the deep pools in the Glass surrendered brownies of eight and ten pounds to his worm. Not so now. All the big fish have gone, fished out or perhaps lost to the habitat changes from forestry in the catchment or the intensification of agriculture. But in the hill lochans they remain, although stunted in size by the peaty acid water and the long winters of icy stupefaction when they are condemned to the bottom in a twilit world of slow motion.

In our eight acres of reflected sky tucked into a wooded hollow on the edge of the moor, Loch Cuill na Caillich (Loch of the Old Woman), the wild brownies are supplemented every spring by North American rainbows we tip in at one and a half to three pounds. A syndicate of local fly fishers who are addicted to whisking away their summer evenings and weekends promptly haul them out again.

We are often given these vigorous firm-bodied fish and Lucinda pops them into the deep-freeze until she has enough to make a fish pie or a kedgeree. Sometimes when the boys are home from university or on summer vacation they drift lazily to the loch and the fishing-hut for long beer-can evenings with occasional bouts of un-energetic fishing from the boats. Brownies or rainbows are cleaned there and then and dropped into a little oil and butter over the hut fire. That is the way to eat trout, in sight of the water they came from and half an hour dead. One of nature's greater delicacies.

Aunt Margaret's Salmon Pie

Ideal for a girls' lunch, served with a salad.

(Serves 6)

Ingredients: pastry
4 oz plain flour
4 oz butter
4 oz grated cheese

Ingredients: filling
1 large tin of salmon (418 g)
1 grated onion
3 eggs
4 oz. grated cheese
1/2 pint sour cream
1 tbs mayonnaise
dill
dash of Tabasco Sauce

Method

Rub the ingredients together and press into a spring form pan or mould, reserving one cup of the crumb mixture.

Combine all the ingredients for the filling and place in the pie shell. Sprinkle the top of the pie with the reserved cup of crumb mixture. Bake in a moderate oven at 180°C/350°F/Gas Mark 4 for 1 to 11/2 hours. Remove carefully from the mould and serve warm with a green salad.

Fresh salmon may be used but the pie is much nicer made with tinned.

Serve a cake plate (Gillie: nicey!)

Salmon Fishcakes with Dill & Egg Sauce

(Serves 4)

Ingredients: Fishcakes
1 lb (450 g) salmon
1/4 pint (150 ml) milk
6 black peppercorns
1 bay leaf
8 oz (225 g) potatoes, peeled
1 oz (30 g) butter
1 egg yolk
1 tsp. finely grated zest from an unwaxed lemon
1 tbsp. finely chopped parsley
salt and freshly ground black pepper
flour, for dusting
vegetable oil, for frying

Ingredients: Dill & Egg Sauce
1 oz (30 g) butter
1/4 pint (150 ml) single cream
2 hardboiled eggs, chopped
2 tbsp. chopped dill
2 tsp. lemon juice

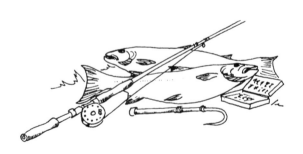

OR See page 160
The Times C. Bk K Stewart

Method

Put the salmon, milk, peppercorns and bay leaf in a saucepan. Bring to the boil, cover and simmer gently for fifteen minutes.

Transfer the fish to a plate, reserving the cooking liquid. When cool enough to handle, remove and discard the skin. Flake the flesh into a large bowl, removing any bones. Mash lightly with a fork.

While the fish is cooking, cut the potatoes into 11/2 inch (4 cm) chunks and cook in boiling salted water for twelve to fifteen minutes, until soft. Drain well and return to the heat for a few seconds to dry. Add the butter and one tablespoon of the reserved cooking liquid from the fish and mash until smooth. Add the potato to the fish together with the egg yolk, lemon zest and parsley. Season with salt and pepper. Mix together lightly, then divide the mixture into four equal portions and shape these into flat cakes on a floured surface. Chill until required.

Meanwhile prepare the sauce: melt the butter in a small pan, add the cream and bring to the boil. Cook, stirring, for two to three minutes until creamy, then add the hard-boiled eggs and dill. Stir in the lemon juice, season and keep warm while cooking the fishcakes.

Heat the oil in a frying pan over a moderate heat. When the oil is quite hot, cook the fishcakes for six to eight minutes until golden brown, turning once or twice.

Serve the cooked fishcakes with the sauce.

Salmon Kedgeree

also leek
celery
Cinuaunch
* mushroom
to make this
dist

Traditionally, a breakfast dish.

(Serves 4 to 5)

Ingredients
4 oz (125 g) left-over cooked salmon, flaked
2 hard-boiled eggs, shelled and chopped
8 oz (250 g) long-grain white rice
1 small onion, very finely chopped
3 oz (75 g) butter
1 chicken stock cube
1 rounded tsp. curry powder
1 rounded tbsp. finely chopped parsley

Method

Cook the rice for ten minutes in a large pan of water, in which you have dissolved the stock cube, until it is just tender. Drain. Cook the onion in the butter in a saucepan over a gentle heat for five to ten minutes or until the onion is soft. Add the curry powder and cook for another couple of minutes, gently fork in the cooked rice, the flaked salmon and the chopped hard-boiled eggs and set aside.

Butter an ovenproof dish liberally and spoon in the kedgeree. Cover with pieces of buttered greaseproof paper or a piece of buttered foil, laid over the top of the kedgeree but not too tightly sealing the contents. Cook in a moderate oven (180°C/350°F/Gas Mark 4) for thirty minutes or until the kedgeree is heated throughout. Just before serving, fork through the finely chopped parsley.

For a special dish, serve with hollandaise sauce. Best served with peas and triangles of brown toast.

Trout en Papillote

(Serves 4)

Ingredients
4 small trout
2 tbsp. finely chopped onion
1/2 lb (250g) button mushrooms, finely chopped
2 tbsp. finely chopped parsley
butter
salt and freshly ground black pepper
4 thin slices lemon
4 tbsp. dry white wine

Method

Clean and prepare the four small trout. Sauté finely chopped onion, mushrooms and parsley in 4 tablespoons of butter until onion is transparent; season to taste with salt and freshly ground black pepper and stuff the fish with this mixture.

Cut four rectangles of foil large enough to envelop the fish completely. Brush the foil with melted butter or olive oil and place the fish in the centre of each piece of foil. Sprinkle each fish with salt and freshly ground black pepper, top with a slice of lemon and pour over 4 tablespoons each of melted butter and dry white wine. Bring the foil up over the top of the fish and double-fold the edges to form a tight pocket. Close the ends of the foil by folding them over and turning them up so that the juices will not run out.

Place on a baking sheet and bake in a moderate oven (190°C/375°F/Gas Mark 4 to 5) for fifteen to twenty minutes. Arrange on a serving dish, slitting the edges of the foil and rolling them back but not removing the fish, because it will fall apart.

MAIN COURSES

Lamb
~

Roddy Miller, a Ranger back in the mid-'70s, cynically named our first orphan lamb "Roast". We found her suckling from her dying mother at the edge of a single-track road many miles up into the mountains. When we returned several hours later, the ewe was dead and the lamb was still weakly attempting to pull milk from the cold corpse. We had not the heart to drive by, so we whisked her tiny form up and wrapped it in a pullover. I think she was about eight hours old when we found her, blood still drying on her umbilical cord.

Roastie lived for thirteen years (a rare age for a Blackface) and had fifteen lambs herself. She grew with my children, who were born more or less with her, so to speak, so that she was always a part of their lives. More than this, she was an indomitable extrovert, running to greet strangers and bleating insistently if she was ignored. On summer evenings, when the warm weather permitted the front doors to be flung open during dinner, Roastie would trot in and disappear beneath the long dining table, where she would thrust her horned head into the laps of astonished guests. Although we tried hard, we never managed to house-train her and the housekeeper did not welcome these visits.

Roastie was only the first. After that, as the children learned to help with the lambing, so year on year they demanded to adopt and bottle-feed any weakling twin or orphan our little flock of Jacobs produced. There were Baba, Mairi, Larry and Fluffy, Skimpy and Gutsy too. A year never went by without another adding its name to the list. Sometimes they stayed pets; usually by winter they had merged back into the flock and were lost to the pressing business of producing lambs themselves. But for the children, as the boxes of butchered meat came back to the deep freezes, the question always lingered.

Home grown lamb or that unfashionable item, mutton (which comes from old ewes no longer able to survive the long winter) is a privilege. Now adult, those same children still beg for lamb chops when they come home. Mutton stews have also fed this family well.

Lamb Boswell

(Serves 4-6)

Ingredients

4 oz butter
2 large onions, finely chopped
8 oz mushrooms
8 oz tomatoes - peeled, de-seeded & chopped
2₁/₂ lb of tender lamb cut into strips
3 oz paprika
2 cloves of garlic, crushed
2 nips of whisky
1/2 pint cream
salt and pepper

Method

Melt half the butter and sauté the onions until they are transparent (not brown). Add the mushrooms and the tomatoes and set aside. Season the lamb and roll in the paprika and garlic. Sauté in the butter and flambé with whisky. Add the cream, onions, mushrooms and tomatoes. Reduce the sauce slightly, correct the seasoning and consistency and serve with rice and a crisp green vegetable.

Lamb Stew with Courgettes

(Serves 4 to 6)

Ingredients
2 1/2 lb boned shoulder of lamb
4 tbsp. olive oil
1 Spanish onion, finely chopped
1 large can peeled plum tomatoes
2 tbsp. tomato paste
2 tbsp. finely chopped fresh parsley
fresh or dried oregano to taste
salt and freshly ground black pepper
2 lb courgettes
4 tbsp. butter

Method

Cut the lamb into 2 inch (4.5 cm) cubes. Heat the oil in a thick-bottomed heatproof casserole and brown the lamb on all sides; add chopped onions and cook until lightly browned. Add the tomatoes and tomato concentrate dissolved in a little water and season to taste with chopped parsley, oregano, salt and freshly ground black pepper.

Bring to a boil; reduce and cover casserole; simmer gently for an hour. Brown courgettes in butter, add them to the casserole and continue cooking for another thirty minutes or until both the meat and the vegetables are cooked.

MAIN COURSES
Pork

~

Old country saying: "Dogs look up to you,
Cats look down on you,
But pigs is equal."

We have lost the pork culture of our forebears. Intensive agriculture and stock rearing methods have no time for beasts of character if their live-weight-gain is low. If a sow cannot produce twenty piglets a year she's no good. It's a tough old world out there if you're a pig at the end of the 20th Century.

It was not always so. There was a time when the pig was as much valued for its recycling ability for household waste, producing the best quality manure for the garden, as for the bacon, ham, sausages and tenderloin roast when the time was right. Every farm and smallholding had one or two, as did every country house and rectory, and every dairy kept pigs to consume the whey. They lived in brick styes with a muddy outrun and in winter were turned out to cleanse a pasture of wire worm and rooty perennials. They were at the very core of country life. They came in every size, colour and shape and with wonderful names such as Wessex Saddleback and Small Dorset Black, Yorkshire White, Tamworth and Flop-eared Hog. Now one only ever hears of Large Whites. Gone too are the smoked bacon sides which hung from kitchen beams, the strings of waxy sausages and whole hams rubbed with saltpetre. Now pigs are fed with fishmeal and corn and reared in heartless incarceration. Bacon comes in packets and sausages are wet and floppy. The industry seems to be in crisis. I am not surprised. If pigs is equal we have a funny way of showing it.

Pork with Cranberries & Orange

(Serves 6)

Ingredients

1.1 kg / 2¹/₂ lb pork tenderloin fillets
1 orange
1 level tbsp. each of chopped fresh rosemary and thyme
or one pinch of each dried herb
1 clove of garlic
salt and ground black pepper
300 ml / 1/2 pint red wine
24 button onions or shallots
6 large celery stalks, with leaves
125 g / 4 oz caster sugar
3 tbsp. port
225 g / 8 oz fresh or frozen cranberries
4 tbsp. olive oil
1 cinnamon stick
2 level tbsp. plain flour
150 ml / 1/4 pint stock
2 level tbsp. chopped, fresh, flat-leaf parsley
25 g / 1 oz unsalted butter

grated orange rind to garnish
Dauphinoise potatoes to serve

Method

Tie the pork tenderloin fillets with string and place them in a deep dish. Grate the orange rind, reserving some to garnish. Squeeze the juice and add 4 tablespoons to the dish, along with the red wine. Add the herbs, crushed garlic and pepper and marinate overnight.

Peel the onions, keeping them whole. Finely chop two level tablespoons of the celery leaves and slice the stalks. Heat the sugar gently until it caramelises but doesn't burn. When it is golden, add the port and cranberries and set aside. Drain the pork, reserving the marinade, and dry the pork on kitchen paper.

Heat half the oil in a casserole dish. Snap the cinnamon stick and add it to the oil. Brown the pork on all sides and set aside. Add the onions to the pan (using more oil if necessary) and fry on a medium heat, stirring continuously, for about ten minutes or until brown. Stir in the flour, celery leaves and reserved marinade. Add the stock and bring the mixture to the boil. Simmer gently for a couple of minutes and return the pork to the pan. Cover and cook at 170°C/325°F/Gas Mark 3 for about half an hour or until the juices run clear when the pork is tested with a skewer.

About ten minutes before serving the pork fry the celery in the butter for three to four minutes.

Meanwhile, take the pork out of the sauce and set aside. Bring the sauce to the boil and bubble for five or ten minutes until thick and syrupy. Add 150ml/1/4 pint of the sauce to the cranberry mixture and bring to the boil. Mix this into the rest of the pork sauce already prepared, adding fresh parsley and seasoning to taste.

Slice the pork and spoon the sauce over to serve, garnishing with the grated orange rind. Serve with the celery and Dauphinoise potatoes.

Pork with Juniper, Celery & Prunes

(Serves 4)

Ingredients
3 tbsp. oil
1½ lb (675 g) pork tenderloin, cut into 1½ inch (3.5 cm) pieces
2 shallots, finely chopped
2 celery stalks, cut into matchsticks
2 tsp. juniper berries, lightly crushed
9 fl oz (250 ml) dry white wine
3 tbsp. sherry
1 bay leaf
4 fresh sage leaves, shredded
12 no-soak prunes
salt and freshly ground pepper
fresh sage leaves, to garnish

Method

Heat the oil in a large saucepan over a high heat. Add the pork and brown on all sides. Using a slotted spoon, transfer to a plate and set aside. Add the shallots to the pan and cook over a moderate heat for four to five minutes to soften. Add the celery and juniper and cook for two minutes. Add the wine, sherry and herbs and bring to the boil. Return the meat to the pan, cover and simmer for twenty minutes. Add the prunes and continue cooking, uncovered, for ten minutes, until the sauce is reduced by about half and the pork is tender. Adjust the seasoning, if necessary, and serve immediately, garnished with fresh sage leaves.

MAIN COURSES

Venison

~

Some say deer are red. It is true that the whole culture of the Highland sporting tradition is built around the red deer. Throughout the 19th Century red deer became an industry in the Highlands, inducing a fashionability endorsed by Queen Victoria herself. After touring the Highlands in 1842 Prince Albert wrote in a letter: *"Scotland has made a highly favourable impression on us both. The country is really very beautiful, although severe and grand, perfect for sports of all kinds..."*

They were hooked. Balmoral Castle, still the Highland Royal residence, was built for them in 1853. With the salmon and a remarkable glut of red grouse, the wild red deer of the native forests and hills of Scotland became the pivotal sporting opportunity which was to create the Victorian world's most celebrated sporting venue.

For 150 years no other species of deer mattered. They were vermin, or just ignored. While princes and dukes were busy glorifying the red deer, the native Highlanders, such as were left in the glens after the mass emigrations to the New World, were happily enjoying for the pot the little roe deer, the other native woodland deer species, which was at times as numerous and widespread as its grand and famous red cousin. It was not, until much later this century when European sporting values began to impact on Britain, that the noble roe, as held by the Germans and Austrians, was valued as a sporting prize. Now the two are almost equals: the red for the open hill stalking and the roe for forest stalking; two entirely distinct sporting disciplines.

While all this was going on, a third species, presented to the Royal Zoological Society in 1860, was introduced from Japan: the sika. It is smaller than the red, with a less dramatic antler formation and is very secretive, preferring dark woods to open country. To begin with they were an interesting novelty for deer park owners around Britain and Ireland. By 1874 they were present in about thirty different parks. Inevitably some escaped into the wild. By the end of the century they were well established as feral deer in woodlands all over the country. What no-one realised was that the sika could interbreed with the wild red deer. Now, at the end of the 20th Century, it is probably the case that no pure-bred red deer exist in mainland Britain any more.

The Highlands' red deer population was slower to become polluted; clearly identifiable hybrids are thankfully rare and are shot on sight. No-one knows the long-term impact of this inadvertent mixing of genes. Paradoxically, from a culinary point of view the picture is not so gloomy.

We think that sika is the best venison of all. Our son Warwick shot a hybrid in the woods a year or two back and it was quite delicious. The meat is sweeter, juicier and does not have the tendency to dry out in the cooking process, as does the meat of the red deer. Roe is also an excellent venison. The problem is simply that the animal is so small that a haunch makes a small joint; best boned and diced for a casserole. So, for sportsmen, deer may still be red, but as for the chef, always happy to see any venison brought into the kitchens, his eyes light up at sika, he smiles broadly for roe, and politely says "thank you very much" for red.

Pot-roasted Venison

(Serves 8)

Ingredients: Roast
5½ lb (2.5 kg) boneless
venison roast
3 oz (75 g) butter
1 large carrot, finely chopped
1 leek or large onion, finely chopped
8 fl oz (250 ml) beef stock
(preferably home-made)
salt
freshly ground black pepper
8 fl oz (250 ml) sour cream
2 slices fresh ginger, chopped
sufficient red wine to cover meat
4 sprigs parsley

Ingredients: Marinade
4 fl oz (120 ml) olive oil
3 cloves garlic, crushed
1 medium onion, sliced
3 cloves
1 bay leaf
1 tbsp. salt
1 tbsp cracked
black pepper peppercorns
1 tsp. dried thyme
1 tsp. allspice or juniper berries
2 slices fresh ginger, chopped

Method

Place the venison in a deep dish or plastic bowl. Combine the ingredients for the marinade and pour over the venison. Cover and leave in the refrigerator for three days, turning now and again. Remove the venison from the marinade and pat dry. Strain the marinade and set aside.

Heat the butter in a large, heavy, flameproof casserole dish and slowly brown the venison on all sides. Add the carrot, leek or onion, three quarters of a pint (450 ml) of the reserved marinade and the beef stock. Season with salt and pepper to taste, cover tightly and bake in a pre-heated moderately slow oven at 160°C/325°F/Gas Mark 3 for 1½ hours, or until the venison is tender. Remove the meat to a platter and keep warm. Reduce the liquid remaining in the casserole by rapid boiling until it measures about 12 fl oz (350 ml). Strain the liquid into a small, clean saucepan, stir in the sour cream and heat through (but do not boil). Taste for seasoning and serve as a sauce with the venison.

Venison Pie

Good quality beef would do.

(Serves 8)

Ingredients

1 1/2 lb (750 g) pickled pork, boned if necessary and cut into chunks
2 lb (1 kg) venison, cut into cubes
1 tbsp. tomato paste
grated zest and juice of 2 medium oranges
1 1/4 pints (750 ml) red wine
beef stock, to cover
salt
1 tbsp. arrowroot
1 tsp. chopped fresh marjoram
shortcrust pastry
1 beaten egg, to glaze

Method

Place the pork in a large saucepan and fry for a few minutes, stirring, until the fat runs. Add the cubed venison and fry until the juice runs and coats the meat with a rich brown gravy (very important). Add the tomato paste, orange zest and juice, add the wine and mix well, scraping up the meat juices and brown bits from the bottom. Add enough stock to cover the meat and salt to taste, allowing for the saltiness of the pork and reduction of the liquid during cooking. Cover the pan and simmer until the meat is very tender (about an hour).

Strain the liquid into a clean pan and thicken to gravy consistency with arrowroot. Add the marjoram, simmer for five to ten minutes and check the seasoning. Place the meat in a large pie dish and cover with the gravy (meat and gravy should come almost to the top of the dish). Roll pastry out to a shape about 1 1/2 inches (4 cm) larger than the top of the dish and cut a strip from the outside to fit around the edge. Dampen the top of the dish, press the strip into place and dampen the top of the strip. Place the top crust into position, press firmly on the strip and trim any excess. Cut a few slits in the top to allow the steam to escape and brush with beaten egg to glaze.

Place in a pre-heated hot oven at 200°C/400°F/Gas Mark 6 for ten minutes, then reduce the heat to moderate (180°C/350°F/Gas Mark 4) and bake for a further thirteen minutes until the pastry is golden.

Baking

~

To this family baking and the late afternoon are an emotional experience, part of the synergy of home life without which nothing would be quite the same. They are as apple blossom is to the orchard, as purple heather is to the hill above the loch in August, as all of us decorating the tree together is to Christmas.

At half-past four no-one has to say "cake" or "scones", "shortbread" or "flapjacks"; the words are redundant. It is axiomatic. Wherever we are on the estate, whatever we are doing: swimming in the loch, collecting firewood in the woods, mending fences and dry-stane dykes or just out and about, our inner compasses wheel us round to head back to the goddess of all afternoon pleasure, the Aga Queen, the matrifocal essence of our home lives, aproned and smiling in the kitchen. That we never know what is the day's offering is part of the ritual. The surprise is seldom a surprise. Lucinda's all-in-one chocolate cake, her gingerbread and her many other culinary delights are all regulars: time-served and approved by decades of ravening children descending like the Assyrian upon the fold.

But you have to be prompt. Late-comers have been known evince silent rage at the empty plates left by their siblings. There is no quarter. A chocolate cake is there to be consumed. In a family of nine one hardly waits to see if anyone is missing. It just goes.

I should hate you to think that this is greed, although I am the first to admit that sometimes the word is not far away. No, it is about a whole rounded sensory experience to which, like circus animals, we have been trained to respond. It is to do with the heady oven aroma overwhelming the kitchen, spilling outside on summer afternoons when all the windows are flung wide; about the spiralling expectation and guesswork as we hurry home through the woods. It is about a quintessential element of home which one can lie back and conjure up when far away in another land, eyes closed, wallowing in the scents, dreaming the salivation of the first bite, smiling the all-enveloping glow of well-being.

Bea's Melting Moments

Ingredients
2₁/₂ oz (65 g) self raising flour
1₁/₂ oz (40 g) caster sugar
2 oz (50 g) margarine
few drops vanilla essence
oats or desiccated coconut
glacé cherries

Method

Cream the margarine, sugar and essence together. Stir in the flour and mix thoroughly. Divide the mixture into twenty pieces, roll each into a ball and toss in oats or desiccated coconuts. Place on a greased baking tray, flatten slightly and place a small piece of cherry on each biscuit.

Bake in a moderate oven at 180°C/350°F/Gas Mark 4 for about fifteen minutes.

Cheese Sablés

Ingredients
2 oz butter
2 oz plain flour
2 oz finely grated Cheddar cheese
*1/2 rounded tsp. mustard **(they never know, but it's a "must"!)***
1 beaten egg
salt and pepper

Method

Rub the butter into the flour until it resembles fine breadcrumbs. Add the grated cheese, mustard, salt and pepper and blend into a dough. Cut into about 20 x 1½ inch (4 cm) rounds. Place on a baking tray and brush with egg.

Cook on a greese proof paper

Bake at 190°C/375°F/Gas Mark 5 for about ten minutes. Leave to cool on the tray for about five minutes before putting them onto a cooling rack, as they are very crumbly.

All-in-one Chocolate Cake

Ingredients: Cake
5 oz self raising flour
6 oz margarine
6 oz caster sugar
3 oz drinking chocolate
(or 1 1/2 oz cocoa powder)
3 large eggs
3 tbsp. boiling water

Ingredients: Icing
4 oz butter
6 to 8 oz icing sugar
1 level tbsp. cocoa
1 tbsp. hot water

Method: Cake

Grease and line an eight inch (20 cm) tin. Mix all the ingredients together and beat for two minutes, allowing lots of air into the mix.

Put the mixture into the tin and bake for about an hour at 180°C/350°F/Gas Mark 4. After removing from the oven, leave in tin for five minutes before turning onto a wire rack to cool.

Method: Icing

Beat the softened butter with a wooden spoon or blender. Gradually beat in sifted icing sugar, a spoonful at a time, then add the cocoa (mixed with the tablespoon of hot water). Add a little milk if required.

Chocolate Brandy Cake

This cake can be made up to five days in advance as it keeps well in the refrigerator. May also be frozen and can double up as a good dinner party dessert.

Ingredients
8 oz (225 g) butter
3 oz (75 g) caster sugar
8 oz (225 g) dark chocolate
8 oz (225 g) digestive biscuits, crushed into crumbs
3 oz (75 g) walnuts, broken into bits
3 oz (75 g) glacé cherries, roughly chopped
2 large eggs
3 tbsp. Brandy

Method

Gently melt the butter and chocolate in a saucepan over a low heat. Stir until well integrated, then allow to cool. Stir in the brandy, crushed biscuits, broken walnuts and chopped cherries. Whisk the eggs and sugar until stiff and pale and fold gently into the chocolate brandy mixture. Line a 2 pint (1.1 litre) loaf tin with siliconised paper as carefully as possible in order to keep the finished cake as neat as possible. Pour the chocolate brandy mixture into the tin, cover with cling film and put into the refrigerator to set. When it has set very hard, run a palette knife down the sides between the paper and the tin, turning the cake onto a plate and peeling off the paper. I like to lay walnut and glacé cherry halves in rows on top.

Date Balls

Ingredients
250 g (9 oz) stoned dates
1 cup sugar
250 g (9 oz) butter
250 g (9 oz) rice crispies (or similar rice-based cereal)
desiccated coconut

Method

Combine all the above ingredients in a heavy-based pot. Stir continuously until all the butter has melted, the sugar dissolved and the mixture has boiled for approximately five minutes.

Add one teaspoon of vanilla essence and 250 g (9 oz) of rice crispies to the mixture. Allow to cool until easy to handle and roll into balls. Dredge with coconut and leave to cool to room temperature.

May be frozen.

Dundee Cake

This is a traditional dish of Dundee, as its name suggests, and to vary the recipe some Dundonians make this cake with half plain to half rice flour.

Ingredients
8 oz butter
8 oz caster sugar
4 to 5 eggs
10 oz sifted flour
1/2 tsp. salt
1 tsp. baking powder
4 oz chopped candied peel
8 oz cleaned currants
8 oz cleaned sultanas
2 oz halved glacé cherries
grated rind of 1 orange
4 oz peeled, blanched almonds

Method

Grease a cake tin, 8 inches (20 cm) across by 3 inches (7 cm) high. Line smoothly with two layers of greased paper. Beat the butter until softened and gradually beat in the sugar. When fluffy add the eggs, one at a time, sprinkling each with a tablespoon of the flour before beating. (If using large eggs, use only four. If medium-sized, use five). Stir in the remaining flour, sifted with the salt and baking powder, then the prepared fruit. Add the orange rind and half the almonds, split or roughly chopped. Mix well. Place in a cake tin and cover with the remaining almonds, split lengthways.

Bake in the centre of a fairly slow oven, 160°C/325°F/Gas Mark 2 to 3 for about three hours, or until dry in the centre when tested with a heated skewer.

Gingerbread

Ingredients
4 oz butter or margarine
4 oz golden syrup
4 oz treacle
1/4 pint milk
4 oz soft brown sugar
8 oz plain flour, sifted
1 tsp. bicarbonate of soda
1 tsp. ground ginger
1 egg

Method

Melt the margarine, sugar, syrup, treacle and milk together, add to the rest of the ingredients and mix thoroughly. Pour into a 2 lb (1 kg) greased and lined loaf tin.

Bake for forty-five minutes to an hour in a moderate oven at 150°C/300°F/Gas Mark 2 1/2 to 3. Store in a tin for two days before cutting (the top will be nice and sticky then).

Ginger Chutney

I have adapted this from a recipe for Indian chutney. I use a little less ginger. These quantities make about 3 lb. We serve this with our cold buffet lunches on Sunday - it should last about two years but never does!

Ingredients
300 g (10 oz) fresh ginger root, shredded
300 g (10 oz) red peppers, diced
250 g (8 oz) cucumber, quartered lengthways and thickly sliced
250 g (8 oz) raisins
250 g (8 oz) onions, roughly chopped
4 lemons, halved lengthways, pips removed, thinly sliced
1 litre (13/4 pints) cider vinegar or white wine vinegar
500 g (1 lb) preserving or granulated sugar
2 tsp. salt

Method

Put all the ingredients, except the sugar and salt, into a large pan and bring to the boil. Reduce the heat and simmer gently for about half an hour, or until the fruit and vegetables have been softened.

Add the sugar and salt to the pan, stirring until they have dissolved, and simmer for a further half an hour to three quarters of an hour, or until the chutney has thickened. Spoon the mixture into hot sterilised jars and seal.

The chutney will be ready to eat in a month, but improves with time.

Nutty Flapjacks

Ingredients
4 oz (100 g) margarine
1 tbsp. golden syrup
4 oz (100 g) sugar
2 oz (50 g) oats
2 oz (50 g) self raising flour
3 oz (75 g) crushed cornflakes

Method

Melt the margarine and syrup over a gentle heat. Mix the dry ingredients and pour on the margarine mixture and mix well. Spread evenly in a greased Swiss Roll tin and press down firmly.

Bake in a moderately hot oven at 190°C/375°F/Gas Mark 5 for about twenty minutes. Cut into fingers whilst warm.

Rosemary Damper

Delicious served buttered, with winter soups.

Ingredients
15g (1/2 oz) butter or margarine
3 cups self-raising flour
2 tbsp. fresh chopped rosemary
1 cup grated cheese
1/2 cup milk
3/4 cup water

Method

Sift flour and rub in butter. Add the rosemary and two thirds of a cup of cheese. Make a well in the centre and stir in the milk and enough water to make a soft dough. Knead on a floured surface until smooth. Place on a greased tray and pat into a 16 cm (5¾ inches) round.

Using a sharp knife, cut 1 cm (1/2 inch) deep slices and sprinkle the remaining cheese over the top.

Bake in the oven at 180°C/350°F/Gas Mark 4 for forty minutes.

(Savoury) Oatmeal Biscuits

A traditional Scottish dish, these are particularly delicious when eaten with cheese.

Ingredients

3 oz butter
3 oz flour
4 oz oatmeal
1/4 tsp. baking powder
1/2 tsp. salt
1 tsp. caster sugar
1 beaten egg
water as required

Method

Rub the butter into the flour and stir in the remainder of the dry ingredients. Add one tablespoon of water to the egg. Make a hollow in the centre of the dry ingredients and add the liquid. Mix to a smooth paste, adding a very little more water as required. Roll out thinly onto a lightly floured board and place a little apart on greased baking sheets. Bake in a moderate oven at 180°C/350°F/Gas Mark 3 to 4 for fifteen to twenty minutes.

(Sweet) Oatmeal Biscuits

Ingredients
1 1/2 tsp. flour
1/4 tsp. salt
1/2 tsp. baking powder
1/2 oz butter
2 tbsp. caster sugar
3 tbsp. golden syrup
1 tsp. vanilla essence
2-3 drops lemon essence
1 beaten egg
1 1/2 cups medium oatmeal

Method

Sift the flour with the salt and baking powder into a basin. Melt the butter in a saucepan. Add the sugar, syrup, vanilla essence, lemon essence and egg. Stir until blended, then gradually beat in the flour mixture and oatmeal. When blended, drop from a teaspoon into rounds, 1 1/2 inches (4 cm) apart, onto a greased baking sheet.

Bake in a moderately hot oven at 190°C/375°F/Gas Mark 4 to 5, for ten to fifteen minutes. Cool on a wire rack.

Scones

Scones are a traditional British tea-time treat. Fresh scones are delicious with cream or butter and jam. Grated cheese may be added to make a savoury scone (add four tablespoons to this quantity). Scones may be kept for a short period in an airtight tin and freeze well.

Ingredients
1 1/2 lb (700 g) self raising flour
1 rounded tsp. salt
2 rounded tsp. sugar (optional)
2 rounded tsp. baking powder
2 eggs
2 tbsp. sunflower seed oil
about 3/4 pint (425 ml) milk

Method

Sieve the dry ingredients together into a large mixing bowl. Beat the eggs and oil in a measuring jug and make up to 1 pint (600 ml) with the milk. Knead the sticky dough which results and press the mixture on a floured surface until it is about an inch (2.5 cm) thick. Use a 2 1/2 inch (6 cm) cutter.

Place the scones onto a greased baking tray and bake in a hot oven at 220°C (425°F/Gas Mark 7) for ten to fifteen minutes.

Seville Marmalade

I usually make my marmalade around Valentine's Day.

Ingredients
2 dozen Seville oranges
5 pints water
7 lb sugar

Method

Peel the oranges and cut the peel coarsely. Reserve the orange pips. Put into the preserving pan with the water, bring to the boil and cover the surface with greaseproof paper. Cover.

Tie the pips in a piece of muslin and soak in 1/2 pint of water overnight.

Add the fruit (cut up), the pips and the warmed sugar. Boil for twenty minutes and then remove the pips and squeeze out the jelly. Continue boiling until the setting point is reached (when a little marmalade is placed on a plate to cool, the surface should wrinkle when pushed with a finger).

Shortbread

Ingredients
1 lb (500 g) plain flour
8 oz (250 g) semolina or ground rice
8 oz (250 g) caster sugar
1 lb (500 g) butter

Method

Mix all the dry ingredients for the shortbread and rub in the butter until the mixture resembles fine breadcrumbs. Press into a shallow 10 x 14 inch (25 x 35 cm) tin. Prick all over with a fork and bake in a slow oven at 150°C/300°F/Gas Mark 2 for about an hour, or until the shortbread is a pale biscuit colour.

Viennese Fingers

Ingredients: Fingers
6 oz (150 g) margarine
2 oz (50 g) caster sugar
6 oz (150 g) self raising flour
few drops vanilla essence
chocolate

Ingredients: Filling
Jam or butter cream

Method

Cream the fat and the sugar together thoroughly and stir in the flour and the vanilla essence. Place the mixture in a piping bag with a large star-shaped nozzle and pipe 2$^{2/3}$ inch (6.5 cm) lengths onto greased baking trays.

Bake in a moderate oven at 160°C/325°F/Gas Mark 3 for about twenty minutes.

When cool, sandwich together with jam or butter cream and dip the ends into melted chocolate to decorate.

Viennese Rosettes: as for Viennese Fingers, but pipe rosettes onto greased baking trays and decorate with a glacé cherry.

(Mrs Bass's) Whisky Cake

Ingredients: Cake
7 oz seedless raisins
3/4 pint water
4 oz cooking fat
5 oz caster sugar
4 oz chopped walnuts
2 tbsp. whisky
1 egg
6 oz plain flour
1 level tsp. bicarbonate of soda
3/4 tsp. ground cloves
3/4 tsp. nutmeg
1 pinch all-spice
1 tsp. salt

Ingredients: Filling
14 oz icing sugar
1 small free range or pasteurised egg
1 tbsp. whisky
2 oz butter

Method: Cake

Grease and line with paper two nine inch (22.5 cm) sandwich tins. Cover raisins with water and simmer for twenty minutes. Drain, saving one third of the liquid, and cool. Cream the fat and the sugar together until light and fluffy and beat in the egg. Sift together the flour, spices and salt. Fold into the mixture alternately with the liquid ingredients. Stir in the raisins, nuts and whisky and pour into the tins.

Bake in a moderate oven at 180°C/350°F/Gas Mark 4 for thirty to thirty-five minutes. Cool on a wire rack and sandwich together with some of the filling, spreading the rest on top.

Method: Filling

Cream the butter and gradually beat in the icing sugar alternately with lightly beaten egg and whisky.

Desserts
~

I prefer the word pudding. Somehow it seems more wholesome than dessert, more homely; right for this harum-scarum country family of animals and muddy trousers. But then I was never very hot on political, let alone culinary correctness. But if it is Queen of Puddings, I don't care what you call it. Just wheel it in, any day of the week, lunch or dinner, sun or moon. Like my horse and my boots, like the dogs and the log fires, Queen of Puddings belongs to the soul of home life, at the very core of good eating. Nor is it alone. All good meals are a balancing act, straddling the tightrope of delight, teetering towards art on one side and over-indulgence on the other. To get it right, with fine wines and as many courses as it takes to produce that abdominal glow we call satisfaction, is a precious gift. Perhaps that is why real restaurants are so ephemeral. Puddings, for all their delectation, must not swamp the other courses, nor vice versa.

If Queen of Puddings reigns supreme, Apple and Bramble Crumble is snapping at its heels, served, as in my Yorkshire youth, with a slice of Stilton cheese. "Apple without cheese is like a kiss without a squeeze", old Nellie used to insist. It also has the added delight of being home-produced: Granny Smiths and Bramleys from the orchard and blackberries from beside the burn, Allt na Caillich, which spills from the loch. Hermione picks the low ones and Lucinda stretches for the fat, sun-reflecting berries the blackbirds have not found.

On other occasions puddings more aptly deserve the term dessert. Lemon Syllabub is one, although the Elizabethan English were less likely to have embraced a borrowed French correctness. This is a refined dish, light and fluffy with the piquancy of white wine and lemon, chilled for summer evenings with fresh strawberries from the Black Isle, sliced as thin as a coin.

What one can say about good food never ends. There is always a surprise, a new dish, an old favourite given a new twist to reflect the occasion or season. Perhaps that is why the subject is so universally popular. It is a part of life as we are so lucky to know it, and one which goes on and on.

Apple & Bramble Crumble

(Serves 4 to 6)

Ingredients: Filling
1 lb (450 g) tart green apples
8 oz (225 g) blackberries
3 oz (85 g) caster sugar
1/2 tsp. ground cinnamon
butter, for greasing
cream or custard, to serve

Ingredients: Topping
6 oz (170 g) flour
3 oz (85 g) butter, diced
2 oz (55 g) Demerara sugar
1 tsp. grated zest from an unwaxed lemon

Method

Preheat the oven to 180°C/350°F/Gas Mark 4 and grease a baking dish with butter.

First prepare the topping: sieve the flour into a mixing bowl and rub in the butter until the mixture resembles fine breadcrumbs. Stir in the sugar and lemon zest and set aside.

Next peel, halve, core and thinly slice the apples. Place the slices in a bowl with the berries, sugar and cinnamon and toss lightly to mix. Transfer the mixture to the prepared dish and sprinkle the crumble mixture over to cover completely. Bake in the oven for about thirty-five minutes, or until the top is golden brown. Serve hot with cream or custard.

Border Tart

(Serves 4 to 6)

Ingredients
shortcrust pastry
2 oz butter
3 oz sugar
1 egg
couple of drops vanilla essence
pinch of baking powder
teacup of mixed dried fruit

Method

Cream the butter and sugar, add the egg and mix well. Add the vanilla essence, baking powder and dried fruit.

Line a flan tin with shortcrust pastry and fill with the mixture.

Bake at 180°C/350°F/Gas Mark 4 for twenty to thirty minutes, or until just set, and serve with ice cream.

Bread & Butter Pudding

(Serves 4)

Ingredients

8 fl oz (250 ml) milk
8 fl oz (250 ml) double cream
pinch of salt
1 vanilla pod
3 eggs
4 oz (125 g) sugar
3 soft bread rolls
1 oz (25 g) butter
2 tbsp. sultanas, soaked in hot water and drained
11/2 tbsp. apricot jam, warmed
icing sugar, to decorate
pouring cream, to serve

Method

Bring the milk, cream, salt and vanilla pod to the boil, then remove from the heat and set aside. Beat the eggs and sugar together in a bowl and stir in the scalded milk and cream mixture. Cut the rolls into thin slices, butter them on one side and arrange in a buttered ovenproof dish, buttered side up. Sprinkle sultanas over the top, then strain the milk and cream mixture over, through a fine sieve.

Place the dish in a roasting pan to serve as a bain-marie, with enough water to come halfway up the sides and bake in a preheated moderate oven (180°C/350°F/Gas Mark 4) for thirty to forty minutes or until puffy on top and set. Spoon warmed apricot jam over and sprinkle with icing sugar.

Serve the pudding warm, with pouring cream served separately.

Chocolate Crispie with Apples & Calvados

(Serves 6 to 8)

Ingredients
6 oz (175 g) golden syrup
6 oz (175 g) butter
6 oz (175 g) good chocolate
5 oz (150 g) cornflakes

Method

Melt the syrup, butter and chocolate together in a double saucepan and pour over the cornflakes. Mix well so that all the flakes are covered in chocolate. Press this delicious chocolatey mass into lightly greased ramekins and hollow up the sides (this mixing should give about six to eight little cases). Leave to cool and set.

Meanwhile, prepare the Calvados cream by whipping 1 pint double cream with about 2 tablespoons of caster sugar and 2 tablespoons of Calvados.

When set, turn the crisps out of the ramekins by running a sharp knife around the edge. Fill the hollows with Calvados cream and apple slices (leaving red or green skin on).

Chocolate Roulade

(Serves 6)

Ingredients: Roulade
5 large eggs, separated
6 oz (175 g) caster sugar
6 oz (175 g) dark chocolate,
broken into pieces
3 tbsp. cold water
put aside 2 oz (50 g) grated chocolate

Ingredients: Filling
8 fl oz (250 ml) double cream, chilled
1 tbsp. icing sugar
dash of vanilla

Method

Grease a baking tray and cover with greased cooking parchment or aluminium foil. Beat the egg yolks and gradually beat in the sugar, continuing to beat until pale and fluffy.

Place the chocolate pieces in a bowl or the top of a double boiler or steamer with the cold water. Set over simmering water and stir until the chocolate melts. Cool a little, then stir the chocolate into the yolk mixture.

Whisk the egg whites until they form soft peaks and fold into the yolk mixture. Spread the mixture evenly on the prepared baking tray, leaving a 1 inch (2.5 cm) margin all round. Place in a pre-heated moderate oven (180°C/350°F/Gas Mark 4) and bake for ten minutes, then reduce heat to (150°C/300°F/Gas Mark 2) and bake for five minutes longer. Remove from oven and cover the top with a cloth which has been wrung out in cold water. Cool, then place in the refrigerator for an hour.

Remove the cloth and loosen the parchment or foil from the baking tray. Dust a large sheet of waxed paper with grated chocolate, turn the roulade out onto the chocolate and carefully peel off the parchment or foil.

Whip the cream with the icing sugar and vanilla and spread half the cream on the roulade. Roll up like a swiss roll, using the waxed paper to help you, and place on a long narrow board or serving platter. Decorate with the remaining whipped cream and, if liked, a few whole strawberries.

Crunchy Cinnamon Pudding

(Serves 4)

Ingredients

8 oz (225 g) fresh breadcrumbs
3 oz (75 g) brown sugar
3 oz (75 g) butter
8 fl oz (250 ml) double cream
4 fl oz (120 ml) water
1 tbsp. sugar
2 tbsp. caster sugar
2-3 tbsp. ground cinnamon
4 cooking apples - peeled, cored & quartered
1 small carton natural yoghurt

Method

Mix together brown sugar, breadcrumbs and cinnamon. Melt the butter in a heavy-based frying pan, add the crumb mixture and stir over a gentle heat until the mixture is crisp and has a toffee-like consistency. Transfer to a plate and cool. Poach the apple in water with the sugar then blend to a soft pureé in a food processor or blender or rub through a fine sieve and cool. Whip the cream with the caster sugar until thick and stir in the yoghurt. In a serving bowl, make a layer of crumbs, alternating with the cream mixture and the sweetened apple and ending with a layer of crumbs. Decorate and serve this dessert very cold.

Lemon Syllabub

An old Elizabethan recipe.

(Serves 6)

Ingredients
8 oz (250 g) fresh sliced strawberries
1/2 pint (300 ml) double cream
juice and grated rind of 2 lemons
1 sherry glass of white wine
2 oz (50 g) caster sugar

Method

Whip the cream, gradually adding the lemon juice, rind, white wine and sugar. When the cream mixture is thick, spoon over the sliced strawberries in the glasses and stir the strawberries up through the lemon syllabub. Chill for several hours before serving.

Prune & Port Fool

(Serves 6)

England is famous for its "fools", a light textured
blend of pureéd fruit with custard or cream.

Ingredients
6 oz (175 g) soft stoned prunes
8 oz (250 ml) water
8 fl oz (250 ml) double cream
4 fl oz (120 ml) port
2 strips of lemon rind
2 tbsp. sugar
A little extra double cream and rind to decorate

Method

Cook the prunes in the water with the rind for about twenty minutes or
until tender. Remove rind and pureé in a food processor or blender or rub
through a fine sieve. Cool and stir in the port. Chill.

Whip the cream and sugar until the mixture forms soft peaks and fold
gently into the prune mixture. Divide into six glasses and decorate with a
spoonful of cream and lemon rind.

Queen of Puddings

(Serves 4 to 6)

Ingredients: Pudding
2 oz fresh white breadcrumbs
1 oz caster sugar
1/2 pint milk
1/2 oz butter
pared rind of 1 small lemon
2 egg yolks
2-3 tbsp. strawberry or raspberry jam, slightly warmed

Ingredients: Meringue
2 egg whites
4 oz caster sugar

Method

Simmer the milk briefly, add the lemon rind and set aside to infuse. Strain the milk into a bowl, add the butter and sugar and, when the sugar has dissolved, the breadcrumbs. Mix and leave to cool. Add the egg yolks, stir thoroughly and turn into a lightly buttered pie dish. Set aside for half and hour, then bake in a moderate oven at 180°C/350°F/Gas Mark 4 for about half an hour, or until set. Remove, allow to cool slightly and spread the jam over the top.

Whip the egg whites until they are firm and white, fold in the sugar and layer the meringue on the top of the pudding. Dust with caster sugar, leave to rest for five minutes and then bake in a slow oven at 150°C/300°F/Gas Mark 2 until the meringue is set and straw-coloured.

Raspberry, Hazelnut & Cinnamon Tart

(Serves 8)

Ingredients: Pastry
4 oz (125 g) plain flour
1 oz (25 g) icing sugar
4 oz (125 g) cold butter
2 oz (50 g) chopped hazelnuts
1 rounded tbsp. ground cinnamon

Ingredients: Filling
3 oz (75 g) sugar
1 lb (500 g) raspberries
1/2 pint (300 ml) double cream,
lightly whipped
1 rounded tbsp. arrowroot

Method

In a food processor blend the chopped butter with the flour, icing sugar and cinnamon until the mixture resembles fine breadcrumbs. Alternatively, rub the butter into the rest of the ingredients with your fingers, until it resembles fine breadcrumbs. Add the chopped hazelnuts and blend for a second or two (just enough to blend the chopped nuts with the rest of the ingredients).

Pat the mixture gently into an eight to nine inch (20-22 cm) flan dish and pop in the refrigerator for an hour to set. Bake in a moderate oven, 180°C/350°F/Gas Mark 4 for half an hour to forty minutes, or until the pastry is golden brown.

Warm the raspberries and sugar together in a saucepan over a low heat until the sugar has dissolved completely in the fruit juices. Mix the arrowroot to a paste with a little cold water in a cup. Stir a couple of spoonfuls of the hot raspberry juice into the cup and then tip the contents of the cup into the saucepan. Stir continuously over a low heat until the sauce boils. As it boils, the raspberry juice will become clear. Remove the saucepan from the heat and set aside to cool. When the sauce has cooled, spoon it into the cooled flan.

Cover with whipped cream, or serve the cream separately.

Rhubarb Charlotte

(Serves 4 to 6)

Ingredients
2 lb rhubarb
1 1/4 lb sugar
3 tbsp. lemon juice
butter
thin slices white bread
brown sugar
whipped cream

Method

Wash and trim young rhubarb stalks and cut into 1 inch (2.5 cm) segments. Combine rhubarb, sugar, lemon juice and 3 tablespoons of butter in a thick-bottomed saucepan. Bring gently to the boil, stirring continuously, and then simmer for about five minutes, stirring all the time, or until the rhubarb is soft but still whole.

Lightly butter a small charlotte mould or soufflé dish and dust with sugar. Trim crusts from the bread; cut enough triangles to cover the bottom of the mould. Clarify butter; dip the triangles of bread into the clarified butter one by one and line the bottom of the mould, overlapping the triangles slightly. Line the sides of the mould with strips of bread in a similar fashion.

Fill the mould with the rhubarb mixture and cover with overlapping triangles of bread dipped in clarified butter. Sprinkle with a little brown sugar and bake in a moderate oven (180°C/350°F/Gas Mark 4) for thirty to thirty-five minutes, or until the bread is golden. Let the mould stand for five to ten minutes after being removed from the oven.

To serve, invert the charlotte onto a heated serving dish. Serve with whipped cream.

APPENDIX - Metric Conversion Table

All recipes are given in imperial measures, with the American equivalent in brackets. The U.K. officially uses the metric system but many cooks, even of the younger generation, still think in imperial!

The following tables give approximate conversions from imperial to metric measures, rounded up or down.

Weights

1/2 ounce (oz.)	10 grams (g.)
1 oz	25g
11/2 oz	40g
2 oz	50g
21/2 oz	60g
3 oz	75g
4 oz	110g
41/2 oz	125g
5 oz	150g
6 oz	175g
7 oz	200g
8 oz	225g
9 oz	250g
10 oz	275g
12 oz	350g

Measurements

1/8 inch (in.)	3 millimetres (mm.)
1/4 in	1/2 centimetre (cm.)
1/8 in	1 cm
3/4 in	2 cm
1 in	2.5 cm
11/4 in	3 cm
11/2 in	4 cm
13/4 in	4.5 cm
2 in	5 cm
3 in	7.5 cm
4 in	10 cm
5 in	13 cm
6 in	15 cm
7 in	18 cm
8 in	20 cm

Weights

1 pound (lb)	450g
11/2 lb	700g
2 lb	900g
3 lb	1kg, 350g

Measurements

9 in	23 cm
10 in	25.5 cm
11 in	28 cm
12 in	30 cm

Volume

2 fluid ounces (fl. oz.)	55 millilitres (ml.)
3 fl oz	75 ml
5 fl oz (1/4 pint)	150 ml
1/2 pint	275 ml
3/4 pint	425 ml
1 pint	570 ml
13/4 pints	1 litre
(2 pint basin = 1 litre)	

APPENDIX - Oven Temperatures

Electric Temperatures	Fahrenheit	Celsius
Very slow	250	120
Slow	300	150
Moderately slow	325-350	160-180
Moderate	375-400	190-200
Moderately hot	425-450	220-230
Hot	475-500	250-260
Very hot	525-550	270-290

Gas Temperatures	Fahrenheit	Celsius
Very slow	250	120
Slow	275-300	140-150
Moderately slow	325	160
Moderate	350	180
Moderately hot	375	190
Hot	400-450	200-230
Very hot	475-500	250-260

APPENDIX - Glossary

(*American equivalent is also often used in the U.K. to mean the same thing).

A

BRITISH	AMERICAN
Anchovy essence	Anchovy paste*
Ashet	Meat dish

B

BRITISH	AMERICAN
Bacon, rashers	Bacon, slices
Baking tray	Cookie sheet
Beetroot	Beets
Belly pork	Pork arm steak
Bicarbonate of soda	Baking soda*
Biscuits	Cookies
Bake blind (*pie case*)	Empty pie shell - line shell with foil and baking beans (*often ceramic*) to pre-cook
Blood heat	Lukewarm (*98.6 degrees Fahrenheit*)*
Boiling fowl	Stewing fowl
Bramble	Blackberry or Blackberry bush
Broad beans	Use fava, lima or java
Bannock	Flat round cakes often made with oatmeal (*i.e. bere bannocks*)
Blaeberries	Bilberries (*alternatively, raspberries or blueberries may be used*)

C

BRITISH	AMERICAN
Cake mixture	Cake batter
Case	Pie shell
Caster sugar	Use granulated sugar
Chilli	Chili pepper
Chipolatas	Cocktail sausages*
Cling Film	Plastic wrap
Cornflour	Cornstarch
Creamed potatoes	Smooth mashed potatoes*
Crisps	Potato chips

D

BRITISH	AMERICAN
Demerara sugar	Light brown sugar*
Digestive biscuits	Graham crackers
Double cream	Whipping cream*
Dripping	Meat drippings

E

BRITISH	AMERICAN
Essence of	Extract of*

F

BRITISH	AMERICAN
Farls	Quarters
Farola	Use milled wheat or semolina
Fats	Shortening*
Frying pan	Skillet*

G

BRITISH	AMERICAN
Gelatine	Gelatin
Girdle	Griddle*
Girnel	Canister or meal chest
Glacé angelica	Candied angelica
Golden syrup	Substitute light corn syrup
Greaseproof paper	Vegetable parchment
Green cured bacon	Unsmoked bacon*
Grill, a	Broiler
Grill pan	Broiling pan
Grill, to	Broil
Gut (e.g. fish)	Clean

H

BRITISH	AMERICAN
Haricot beans	Navy or white beans
Hodgils	Oatmeal dumplings

I

BRITISH	AMERICAN
Icing	Frosting
Icing sugar	Confectioners' sugar

J

BRITISH	AMERICAN
Jam	Preserves
Jelly bag	Use several layers of cheesecloth*
Joint *(of meat)*	Roast *(of meat)*

K

BRITISH	AMERICAN
Kail	Kale *(Scottish: Kale)*
Kippers	Kippered herrings
Kitchen paper/Paper towels	Kitchen towels*
Knead/knock back *(dough)*	Punch down
Knuckle of veal	Veal shanks

L

BRITISH	AMERICAN
Lettuce, a	Lettuce, a head of
Liquidizer/Mixer	Blender/Mixer

M

BRITISH	AMERICAN
Middle neck of lamb	Neck of lamb*
Mince, to *(e.g. minced beef)*	Grind, to *(e.g. ground beef)*
Mixed spice	Allspice*

P

BRITISH	AMERICAN
Pigeon	Squab
Pinhead oatmeal	Irish oatmeal
Plain flour	All-purpose flour *(see also "Strong Plain Flour")*
Preserving sugar	Substitute granulated sugar
Prove	Rise
Pudding	1. Dessert *(colloquial)* More specifically, a steamed, baked or boiled dish, often cooked in a pudding basin i.e. Christmas Pudding. May also be meat or vegetable based, e.g. Haggis.
Pudding basin	Mold or ovenproof bowl
Pudding cloth	Cheesecloth*

R

BRITISH	AMERICAN
Rashers of bacon	Slices of bacon
Ratafia biscuits	Substitute almond flavoured cookies or dried macaroons

S

BRITISH	AMERICAN
Salt Beef	Corned Beef Brisket
Scrag end neck of lamb	Neck of lamb*
Self-raising flour	All-purpose flour sifted with baking powder
Strong plain flour	Unbleached white flour
Seville oranges	Substitute sliced naval/Florida oranges, adding one thinly sliced lemon
Shredded suet	Chopped beef suet
Sieve, to	Sift*
Single cream	Light cream
Soft brown sugar	Use light brown sugar
Spring onion	Scallion*/green onion
Stalk	Remove stalks*
Stewing steak	Braising beef
Stick celery	Celery stalk*
Stoned raisins	Seedless raisins*
Streaky bacon	Use regular bacon
Sultanas	Seedless white raisins
Spurtle	Wooden spoon or spatula

T

BRITISH	AMERICAN
Tartlet tin	Muffin pan
Top and tail	Take ends off/clean (e.g. gooseberries)
Treacle	Molasses

W

BRITISH	AMERICAN
Whisk	Beat/whip*
Wholemeal	Wholewheat

AIGAS FIELD CENTRE

"Man has suffered in his separation from the soil and the other living creatures of the world; the evolution of his intellect has outrun his needs as an animal, and yet he must still, for security, look long at some portion of the earth as it was before he tampered with it." **Gavin Maxwell.**

As well as being a family home and working estate, **Aigas** is the Highlands' principal field studies centre. For over 25 years we have been running programmes for groups seeking a very special Highland experience. Our specialist service designs programmes to meet the needs of your society, institute or organisation. Subjects cover the history of the land, its structure and geology, its wildlife, people and their turbulent history. We can arrange an entire programme for you by fax or e-mail, designed to your transport requirements, blend of topics, and to match your budget, including Shetland, Orkney, the Western Isles and Skye as well as the entire Scottish mainland. **Aigas** is readily accessible: only 25 minutes from Inverness railhead and airport.

Aigas has a team of qualified staff and excellent facilities: comfortable heated accommodation with private bathrooms for up to 40; lecture room, library, dining hall and shop. Outside, the grounds contain three miles of nature trails, a loch, native woodlands and gardens. We also have negotiated access to 700 square miles of mountain, forest, glens and moors. There are over 150 species of birds; and pine martens, deer, otters, dolphins and seals, all within easy reach. We visit historical and archaeological sites, coastal and marine habitats as well as a broad range of woodland, wetland and moorland habitats.

We pride ourselves in high standards. Our aim is to encourage environmental awareness through enjoying and learning about the Highlands and Islands. Visitors from all over the world have been welcomed here. We hope you will come and join us too.

Aigas Field Centre, Beauly, Inverness-shire, IV4 7AD
Tel: 01463 782443   Fax: 01463 782097
E-mail: info@ aigas.co.uk Web: http://www.aigas.co.uk